Old ELLON

by

Linda Birnie

Aberdeenshire

COUNCIL

This book has been published
in association with Aberdeenshire Council.

Commercial Road is situated in the western part of Ellon and formed part of the town's westward expansion during the mid-nineteenth century. Industries including a slaughterhouse, marts and a boot factory were also opened in the area and created a demand for housing for attendant workers.

FURTHER READING

The books listed below were used by the author during her research. None of them are available from Stenlake Publishing. Those interested in finding out more are advised to contact their local bookshop or reference library.

Godsman, James, *A History of the Burgh and Parish of Ellon, Aberdeenshire*, 1958

Goring, Rosemary, ed., *Chambers Scottish Biographical Dictionary*, 1992

Macleod, Revd N. K., *Ellon Castle, With Notes on Abbotshall and Waterton*, reprinted from *The Castles of Buchan*, originally published 1895

Ord, J., *The Bothy Songs and Ballads of Aberdeen, Banff & Moray, Angus and the Mearns*, 1930

Pratt, J. B., *Buchan*, Heritage Press, 1978 (facsimile reprint of original 1858 publication)

Rennie, B., *The Latter Day Horse Dealers*, Aikey Fayre, 1994

Rennie, B., *The Horseman's Word*, Aikey Fayre, 1994

Scott, Revd W. M. F., ed., *The Vale of Ythan: Book of the Bazaar*

Ellon Skweel, 100 Years, Ellon Academy, 1976

Ellon Times

'The Big Roup, For Sale "Practically the whole town of Ellon"', Bob Smith, *Leopard Magazine*

'Bloody Battles and Secret Gardens', Linda Tyler, *Leopard Magazine*, January 1989

'Changes at the Castle', Lucy Gordon, *The Advertiser*, 1 December 2000

'Ellon's Hospital of 100 Years Ago', Linda Tyler, *The Advertiser*, 21 October 1988

'Focus on Ellon', Bob Smith, *Leopard Magazine*

'The Ythan: A River of History', Dave Raffaelli, Newsletter of the Ellon and District Historical Society, March 2002

ACKNOWLEDGEMENTS

The author would like to thank the staff of Ellon Library for their invaluable help in providing research materials for this book, as well as local people who shared their memories and helped with background information. The publishers would like to thank Jenny Hyland of Ellon Library for reading the manuscript, and David Catto of Aberdeenshire Library and Information Service for making pictures from the John Morrison Collection available for use in the book. These appear on the inside front cover, pages 2, 13, 20 (upper), 25, 29, 32 (upper), 33, 36 (lower), 40 (upper and lower), 45, 48, inside back cover and back cover.

INTRODUCTION

The Parish of Ellon lies to the west of Tarves and Methlick Parishes, with Udny and Logie Buchan to the south and south-west, Cruden to the east, and Old and New Deer to the north. It measures roughly eight-and-a-half by five-and-a-half miles, and has an area of 23,137 acres.

The name Ellon has been the source of much debate. In the newsletter of the Ellon and District Historical Society of October 2003, Alan Cameron suggests that it derives from *eilean*, the Gaelic word for island, which is pronounced with the emphasis on the first syllable and is how a good Buchan tongue would pronounce Ellon. Godsman (*A History of the Burgh and Parish of Ellon*) notes that the *Book of Deer* refers to it as 'Helan', while other examples are 'Helin' in 1165 and 'Elone' in 1328. The Ythan contains many islands, including one at Waterton, illustrated on the inside back cover, which would support this theory.

The first known written record of Ellon appears in the *Book of Deer* in 1132. On 10 August 1157, Pope Adrian IV confirmed to the See of Aberdeen the lands in Ellon held by Master Philip, now called Dudwick. In 1165 'the lands of Helen which Sloagth held' were granted to the bishop, prior and convent of St Andrews, which also held Fortrie of Esslemont, part of Waterton, Knockothie and Balmacassie, plus riggs, tenements and gardens in and around Ellon and the lands of Ardgight, Clayhills and Kermucks.

In 1265 Gameline, Bishop of St Andrews, leased his land of 'Elon' to Alexander Comyn, Earl of Buchan, for a rent of two merks of silver per annum. These are known as the Scoloc lands, and their connection with St Andrews indicates that Ellon was both a place of some importance and a leader in sophisticated Christian worship. It was determined in 1387 that the Scoloc lands had a yearly value of £15.13s.4d. The tenant of the lands had to provide 'four clerks with copes and surplices able to read and sing sufficiently', plus housing for the scolocs, 24 wax candles three times a year, and a smithy at Ellon. It has been suggested that the word 'scoloc' may have related to 'scholar', and initially the scolocs had a 'definite educational status' (Godsman), although this appears to have become less significant by the late fourteenth century.

By the start of the seventeenth century, Ellon and the surrounding area was controlled by a number of influential lairds, all with significant land holdings. These landlords were the Gordons of Ardlethen, the Forbes of Waterton, the Errols of Esslemont, the Gordons of Fechil, the Udnys of Udny and the Annands of Auchterellon. Ellon was granted burgh of barony status in 1707 by Queen Anne, helping its economy develop by allowing markets to be held and goods to be sold to customers outwith the local area. Markets took place on the first and third Mondays of the month, and also at Marymas Fair (held in August), the Feast of the Nativity of the Blessed Virgin, and Rude Fair in May.

Describing the town in 1721, an Episcopalian minister wrote: 'Ellon is pleasantly situated on the river. There is a large toll booth and a large building for a tavern, far exceeding any other of that kind in Buchan.' He continued with a description of the 'great and stately castle of Ellon', adding that the River Ythan 'abounds with salmon, trout and many other kinds of fish' and stating its importance to the local economy.

In the years prior to 1750, a variety of professions and trades were represented in the town. The professional classes included a notary public, town clerk, the factor to the Laird of Ellon and a bailiff. Among the tradesmen were a shoemaker, tailor, six merchants, a mason, wright, builder, joiner and sculptor. Situated in the midst of crofting and farmlands, the economy of Ellon was of course hugely dependent on agriculture, while farmers relied on the town for the provision of goods and services:

> The very King that wears the crown,
> The brethren of the sacred gown,
> And Dukes and Lords of high renown,
> Depend upon the ploughmen.

Ellon's citizens were generally supporters of the 1745 Jacobite uprising, and many of them would have fought at Culloden. William Wilson, tailor, made some of the Highlanders' garments and 'followed them north for payment'. Merchants including George Leggat and William Mill 'always kept rejoicing when the rebels [Jacobites] met with success'. Part of Bonnie Prince Charlie's army crossed the ford at Ellon under the command of Lord George Murray, Lieutenant General of the Jacobites, and received good Buchan hospitality. They would have continued northwards via New Pitsligo and Banff. The kirk records of April 1746, following the battle of Culloden, relate that 'the sacrament is delayed beyond its usual time', while concern was expressed at 'seeing the nation so unsettled by reason of the mischievous and unnatural rebellion'.

The presence of a ford across the River Ythan was one of the key factors in Ellon's growth and development. The Ythan rises in Forgue Parish at the Wells of Ythan, and after a 30-mile course flows into the North Sea at Newburgh, sometimes referred to as Ellon's port. Once noted for its pearl oyster fisheries, the river is mentioned in unpublished legislation dating from the reign of Charles I which refers to 'repeating the patent for the pearl-fishery in the Ythan, granted to Robert Buchan'. The same source (*Buchan*, by J. B. Pratt) cites the *New Statistical Account* as '[giving] countenance to a prevalent tradition that the large pearl in the crown of Scotland was procured in the Ythan'. This pearl was said to be gifted to James VI in 1620 by Sir Thomas Menzies of Cults. Skene, author of *A Succinct View of Aberdeen*, says it was 'for beauty and bigness, the best that was at any time found in Scotland'. Today the Ythan, its estuary and the area encompassing the Sands of Forvie remain important wildlife habitats of worldwide scientific interest.

In his 1841 *Statistical Account* of the parish of Ellon, the Revd James Robertson notes that 'The tenure of the lands of Kenmuick, now called the lands of Ellon in this parish, may have some interest for the antiquary. There is attached to the proprietorship of these lands the heritable office of constable of Aberdeen. This office, which at one time was of considerable dignity and importance, is probably as old as the thirteenth century, when the Castle of Aberdeen would seem to have been built. The lands of Kenmuick or Ellon are now in the possession of the Honourable William Gordon, second son of the late Earl of Aberdeen; but the name of the old family of Kenmuick, probably one of the oldest in this part of Scotland, was Kennedy or Kemptie.'

In fact the office of Constableship of Aberdeen was one of Culloden's casualties. Efforts to return the Stuarts to their ancient throne led to government policy that was 'injudicious, and calculated to exasperate the public mind' (Pratt, p230). The following legislation was introduced: 'All heritable jurisdictions of justiciary, and all regalities and heritable bailieries, and all heritable constabularies, other than the office of High Constable of Scotland, and all stewartries being parts only of shires or counties, and all sheriffships and deputy sheriffships of districts, being parts only of shires or counties within Scotland, belonging unto or possessed by any subject, and all jurisdiction and privileges thereto appurtenant, shall be, from and after the 25th day of March 1748, totally dissolved and extinguished.'

Writing about Ellon's church in his 'View of the Diocese', Pratt notes:

'Ellon hath the blessed Virgin Mary for its tutelary [guardian]. The patronage belongeth to the Earl of Aberdeen, who had it from Waterton, who had it from the Earl of Elgin; who got it with the other patronages belonging to Kinloss Abbay [sic]'. The building that replaced the old church in 1777 was described in the *New Statistical Account* by Revd Robertson as follows: 'The Parish Church . . . is a very plain erection, quite in the usual style of Scotch country churches . . . Although it can boast . . . of no architectural beauty, it is a commodious and comfortable place of worship'. Elsewhere he states that: 'The kirk and kirk lands of Ellon belonged to the Cistercian Abbey of Kinloss in Moray. It is probable they were conferred on this abbey at its foundation, in the middle of the twelfth century. They certainly belonged to it in the thirteenth century, as we find that, at an early period of the century following, Robert I confirmed to the abbot of Kinloss, the advocation and donation of the Kirk of Ellon. The Kinloss monks probably acquired Ellon from one of the earliest Earls of Buchan. The Buchan family seem to have been partial to the Cistercian order, as they founded and endowed an abbey of this order at Deer.'

Towards the end of the eighteenth century, trade in cattle, grain, coal, lime, bone-dust and other commodities is recorded, with no less than £100 per week said to be paid by Aberdonian merchants for stockings knitted in the parish. This was work that could be carried out by men, women or children, and could be done in the poor lighting afforded by a peat fire or rush-wicked lamp. Little capital was required and the skill could readily be learnt. Spinning was also undertaken, with four looms worked.

Life in Ellon focused on the Moot Hill, where three times a year a head court was led by the Thane of Buchan, supported by his heavily armed retainers and attended by his vassals. They in turn were accompanied by their retainers, who were also armed. Pratt describes Ellon as 'the heart which sent its pulses [to] every corner of the district'. Penal trials and executions took place in the town, which was a place of 'metropolitan importance'.

Despite periodic fluctuations in its fortunes, Ellon has flourished as a trading centre for a surrounding rural hinterland for many centuries now, and continues to serve this purpose today alongside a new role as a dormitory town for workers in Aberdeen.

This picture and the following four show Ellon Castle and its grounds. Writing in 1895, the Revd N. K. Macleod suggested that the ruins situated on the terrace at Ellon Castle were remnants of a structure called the Abbotshall, built by Abbot Thomas Chrystall in 1532. The ancient name of the site on which the ruins stand was Ardgight (also known as Ardgirth or Ardith). This area was additionally known as the Candle Lands because of the obligation of the occupier or tenant to supply 24 wax candles three times a year to burn before the high altar of the Church of Ellon. In 1559 the Candle Lands were leased by Walter Reid to Alexander Bannerman of Waterton, but Abbotshall was specifically excluded from the lease. Godsman, writing in 1958, is of the opinion that the ruins by the castle are not the remains of Abbotshall at all. He cites the style of masonry and presence of gun loops as evidence for this, and also refers to a map of *c.*1650 by Gordon of Straloch which identifies Abbotshall as being downriver of Ardgirth. The picture is complicated by the frequent name-changes recorded in and around Ellon. Others maintain that the ruined tower fortalice is a replica of the Abbotshall of Kinloss, which was built by Thomas Chrystall's successor, Abbot Robert Reid, later Bishop of Orkney.

Abbotshall of Ellon subsequently passed into the ownership of the Kennedys of Kinmucks, and they are thought to have changed the name to Kinmucks (records exist of Ellon Castle being called Kermucks). In 1652 a dispute arose between Forbes of Waterton and the Kennedys despite previously co-operative and friendly relations. The then Kennedy laird wanted to cut a fourteen-foot deep channel across the Peterhead road near the site of the East Lodge of Ellon Castle between Waterton and Ellon, allowing him to erect a mill. This would have involved rerouting the Modley Burn to a small loch within the lands of the castle, hence the need for the ditch. Not only would the work have stopped traffic on the public road for some weeks, but the mill would have competed with Forbes's existing milling enterprise. Forbes and his neighbours obtained a legal interdict called a civil interruption which was read by Forbes to Kennedy on 12 February 1652. This seemed to settle the matter, but around noon the following day Kennedy and his servants started work on the ditch. The laird was carrying 'ane prodigious great twa handed sword', and his family and staff were also armed. Scarcely had Kennedy started to dig when Forbes, also bearing arms, attended the scene, along with the Sheriff Clerk of Banff. Forbes had been advised that should the interdict be ignored 'to have persons readie with shooles and spades to cast in what should be digged furth'. There was a clash, which Mr Paterson, the minister, was able to calm for a short time. However, fighting soon broke out again and a stone knocked out three of Kennedy's teeth. He then took the two-handed sword to Forbes and 'cleft through his skull and mininges'. The sheriff was severely injured and Forbes was mortally wounded, lingering in a paralysed state until his death four months later. As a consequence the Kennedys became outlaws and the Moirs of Stoneywood took over their lands.

The Moirs sold the Kennedy lands to Sir John Forbes of Waterton in 1668. He married Jane Gordon of Haddo, sister of the 1st Earl of Aberdeen, and their son eventually sold the property on to Bailie Gordon, a merchant of Bordeaux and native of Bourtie who lived in Edinburgh. He added a large hall to the fortalice, designed by Baxter of Edinburgh. Gordon's two sons were murdered by their tutor, the boys having reported 'some liberties they saw him take with their mother's maid'. The tutor was apprehended by an angry mob whose members had witnessed the murders, and was executed two days later. A cube sundial in memory of the boys stands in the grounds of the castle. Bailie Gordon is said to have felt uneasy owning Ellon, as it had mostly been church property, and in 1770 he sold it to George Gordon, 3rd Earl of Aberdeen, along with the lands of Waterton. George kept a mistress, Penelope Dering, at the castle, and their two children were raised there. He had a further two mistresses at the same time as Penelope, and they lived in Cairnbuig Castle and at Wiscombe Park. Lord Aberdeen built two wings on to the castle and eventually died there in 1801. His second son, Hon. William Gordon, inherited Ellon, but never lived there, allowing trees in the grounds to be felled and the house to fall into disrepair. It was pillaged during this period, with marble mantelpieces and other valuables stolen, and the yew garden and terrace planted with potatoes. William Gordon left Ellon to his half-brother Alexander, a cavalry officer who had fought in the Peninsular War. Alexander became known as the 'auld laird' and was initially famed for his benevolence. He lived almost entirely at Ellon.

At first there was harmony between Alexander Gordon, his tenants and the villagers. The latter asked for a site for a town hall and not only was their request granted but the hall was also built by the laird. In 1853 100 of Alexander Gordon's tenants presented him with a portrait painted by Sir John Watson Gordon 'to be retained in his family as an heirloom that it may lead the generations that succeed him to cherish the same friendly sentiments towards the tenantry as he had never failed to manifest to them'. These feelings of esteem wore a little thin, however, when the tenants' leases expired and new buildings were only allowed to be constructed on payment of 30 years' ground rent, after which ownership of the buildings reverted to the laird. During his stewardship, a reconstruction plan was drawn up for Ellon Castle involving rebuilding on the same plateau, further to the east, retaining only the original fortalice. Construction of the newer section of the castle was so solid that gunpowder was a necessary element of the remodelling work, but in the absence of Alexander Gordon, workmen were over-liberal with the explosives and rather more of the existing structure was taken down than had been planned. The same Gordon was also responsible for laying out the 'Roza Walk', named after his daughter-in-law, the late Mrs George Gordon of Ellon. This ran along both sides of the river from the Meadows to Mains of Waterton. The rocky banks were graced with trees, broom, bracken, wild rose, heather, honeysuckle and other wild flowers, and walkers could glimpse views of the Ythan Estuary, the sea and the Forvie sands.

By the time Alexander died in 1873 the family finances were in poor shape, not helped by the 1865 agricultural depression. The castle lay unoccupied until the early 1880s when his grandson, Arthur Gordon, succeeded to Ellon, by which time an onerous mortgage was in place. In 1913 he signed the lands over to trustees and the castle was then let to Major Ian Bullough. The greater part of it was demolished in 1929. Sir Frederick Becker converted what remained – the stables and the servants' quarters – into a modern residence which was then purchased by Sir Edward Reid. His father, Sir James (see page 36), had been Queen Victoria's physician, and he remained there until 1973 when the property was sold to a Mr MacDonald. Eleven years later proposals were put forward to convert the castle to a luxury hotel. Objections were raised and the plans did not go ahead, but virtually all the grounds were sold to make way for the building of the health centre, the new part of Ellon Academy and a housing estate. The modernised castle now comprises four reception rooms, seven bedrooms, five bathrooms and four acres of grounds, while the Ellon Castle Gardens Trust now has an extended lease on the formal gardens. There is reputed to be a tunnel that leads from the castle, under the terrace and the River Ythan to the old rectory of St Mary's on the Rock. The tunnel is also said to lead to the site of a former convent, located where the 'Merc' Hotel (formerly the Craighall Hotel, Mercury Motor Inn and Craighall Lodge) stands today. The West Lodge, a gatehouse to the castle, dates from 1889 and was formerly known as 'Bremner's Lodge', as for 50 years it was home to George Bremner, gamekeeper. It remained unoccupied after Barratt Construction used it as a site office in 1976 and until recently stood unused in the grounds of Ellon Academy. It has now received an architectural award, having been moved stone by stone and resited as a dwelling on the south side of the Ythan.

Ellon grew up around the main ford across the Ythan on the route north from Aberdeen to Peterhead and Fraserburgh. Parish records of 1616 record that efforts were then being made to raise funds to build a bridge over the Ythan at Ellon. However, it was not possible to obtain the money and many years passed before building began. A letter from Lord Saulton of 24 November 1790 on behalf of the Commissioners of Deer District discusses the raising of subscriptions to build a bridge. The project, which went ahead shortly afterwards, was supported by Ellon presbytery, and the bridge's location was determined by the 3rd Earl of Aberdeen, resident of Ellon Castle.

The road trustees agreed to construct the Aberdeen to Peterhead turnpike 'to suit the locality chosen by his lordship for the bridge', and in 1793 the three-arched stone and lime structure was completed. A stagecoach service was subsequently introduced, calling at the New Inn and taking passengers to outlying towns and villages. This remained operational until the arrival of the railway in 1861 when it was withdrawn.

Ellon is often referred to as 'the gateway to Buchan', and indeed it was the chief town of the Pictish province of Buchan as early as 400 BC. The Moot Hill, topped with a motte and bailey castle, was the legal and civil nerve centre of Buchan, and was built near the ford across the river, presumably to protect it. Much of the route of the modern A92 was once a track made by cattle walking to the marts in Aberdeen, sixteen miles southwards, and by the folk of Buchan going about their business. Despite the age of tarmacadam, some of the twists and turns of the drove road remain, although straightening and widening have of course taken place and what was once a day's journey to Aberdeen is now a fifteen-minute drive.

The original bridge was superseded by a more modern structure built in 1939–40, although its 1793 predecessor remains in position (sealed off to traffic). Famously associated with Ellon Bridge is Johnny Ramensky (1905–72), also known as Johnny Ramsay. He was a convicted safe-breaker of Lithuanian extraction whose vocation was, it seemed, compulsive safe-, bank- and jail-breaking. He escaped from Peterhead prison five times and from Barlinnie several times, and was known by police as 'Gentle Johnny' as he never threatened them with violence. Johnny enjoyed strong public sympathy and eventually died in Perth prison. On one escape, Ramensky is said to have successfully crossed underneath Ellon bridge, hand over hand, while police officers guarded the crossing.

Bridge Street. An important stage in the development of modern Ellon took place when Alexander Gordon inherited the castle and its lands from his half-brother, William, in 1845. The following year he extended the castle's West Avenue from the old road leading over Market Hill, connecting it with the road to Deer. Around the same time development also took place in Bridge Street, Langley Road (which was to become Station Road) and the New Deer road. The Chestnuts on Bridge Street dates from 1845–7, and Cosy Neuk was also built in this period by Thomas Milne Snr., who died there in 1857. They have both since been split into smaller flats. A brewery built by a Mr M'Glashan on the west side of Bridge Street later became Neil Ross's garage and is seen on the right here.

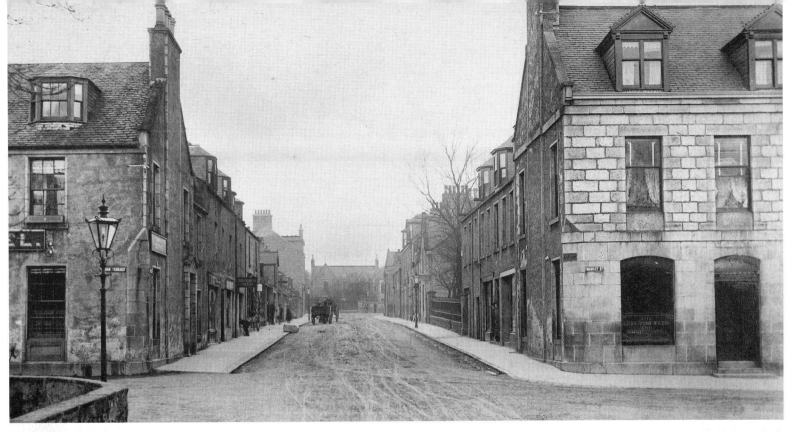

Bridge Street, the main shopping street in Ellon, is lined with a mixture of shops and cottages but used to be dominated by Neil Ross's business, which sold tractors and cars and incorporated a repair garage. Originating from Aboyne, Neil came to Ellon in 1917, opening a bike shop on 7 May that year. He had originally been a farm labourer, and earned £4 for his first six months work. Neil took a correspondence course in mechanics and electrical engineering, studying by candlelight. He was quoted as saying 'A'body thinks I got on because I worked hard – it's nae so – I got on because a didna like farm work'. His studies eventually gave him the skills to install an electric light to replace the candle. The farmer he worked for was unimpressed, however, and blamed 'the magic light' whenever his animals were sick. Neil worked from 8 a.m. to the early hours of the morning for many years building up his cycle business, and then bought the old brewery building which became the Ellon Motor Works. A filling station stood in the Square (now the site of Toymasters) which he bought in 1926 and which featured four electric pumps and one hand-operated pump. From the 1930s Neil had a car showroom, tractor and machinery department, then after buying the former boot factory by Gareta Hill (see page 36) he ran a tractor repair business from it. He was a major employer in Ellon, with branches of the business as far afield as Elgin, Orkney and Shetland. Neil Ross died aged 80 on 23 December 1970, and the business continued for a further ten years before it was sold. Today the name Neil Ross Square serves as a permanent reminder of a farm-hand turned entrepreneur.

Ellon was originally centred around the Square, with the manse and parish church to the east. George Gordon, 3rd Earl of Aberdeen, took on patronage of the church, which was rebuilt in 1777 on the site of a twelfth-century predecessor. This had stood on an ancient sacred site which is marked by a Pictish symbol stone. The Church played a vital role when Ellon was hit by severe food shortages in the eighteenth century. On 27 January 1740 it was recorded that 'the poor in the parish were in a most deplorable condition through the continuance of the violent season and scarcity of victuals'. In 1782 the kirk session bought 60 bolls of beer and pease meal at sixteen shillings to feed 110 needy householders. The old church's capacity was insufficient for the congregation, with tents erected on occasion to accommodate overspill from Communion services. The fabric of the building was a cause of concern for years prior to its replacement, something that attracted the attention of a soothsayer, Thomas the Rhymer, who predicted its collapse on an unidentified Pasch Sunday. He foretold that the fall of the church would be preceded by the presence of a white bull in the churchyard. On Pasch Sunday 1776, a member of the congregation in the west gallery looked out of the window behind him to see a white stirk grazing the churchyard. In his fear, he exited the church Tarzan-style via the window by means of a bell rope! Apart from a torn coat and the loss of a few teeth he was unscathed, although the event brought worship to an abrupt halt as the terrified congregation fled the church. Despite the panic the building did not collapse: indeed, a hefty application of gunpowder was needed to demolish it when it was rebuilt the following year. Ellon Parish Church was restored in both 1829 and 1876, and further upgrading took place from 1907 onwards.

Bailie Gordon bought Ardgirth from Sir John Forbes in 1706 and his widow sold the estate to George, 3rd Earl of Aberdeen in 1752. The Gordon coat of arms may be seen on the south wall of Raeburn, Christie & Co. in the Square. It features a boar's head, grapes and the motto *Veniunt Felicius Uvae* meaning 'Grapes Come with Good Fortune'. It is likely that the arms were resited from the porch at the castle, and they are now positioned close to where the original tolbooth, built in 1706, would have stood. The tolbooth, which was probably similar in appearance to Kintore Town House, stood as a symbol of law and justice. It was situated end-on to the Square with a double external flight of stone steps leading to the first floor, and incorporated a jail, with offenders tried and sentenced by the kirk session in front of the jail and made to sit there on Sundays on public view. They would be clad suitably in sackcloth, bare legged and with bare feet and half-shaven heads. At basement level were girnals, receptacles for oatmeal which was a means for some of paying rent. There was also an area known as the 'salmon house'. The water trough within the Square was gifted to the Burgh of Ellon in memory of Eleanor Vere Boyle (1825–1916) 'For the refreshment of weary beasts'. Eleanor Boyle, nee Gordon, was a daughter of the castle and a distinguished artist known by her initials EVB. There being few weary beasts in Ellon these days the trough now contains flowers. Also located in the Square is the war memorial, which takes the form of a Gordon Highlander and bears plaques with the names of those local people who have paid the ultimate price in war. In 1845–7 the Town & County Bank was built in the Square by John Rae Jnr. The New Inn lies to the west of the Square and Ellon Castle to the north.

Ellon's Square was the location of feein' markets, a form of labour exchange where farmers and farm workers would mingle in order to meet the needs of employees and employers. The feein' markets marked a 'term' of six months, a long time if a poor match was made. Payment was at least partly withheld until the term had expired and local tradesmen were used to offering some form of credit until the term came round. The process has been recorded in the bothy ballad *Ellon Fair*.

Twas in the merry month of May
When flowers had clad the landscape gay,
To Ellon Fair I bent my way
With hopes to find amusement.

A scrankie chiel to me cam near
An quickly he began ti spear
If I wad for the niest half year
Engage to be his servant.

Market Street. On the north bank of the Ythan, slightly west of the ford and opposite the New Inn on Market Street, is the site of Ellon's former Motte or Moot Hill. This was a Norman earthwork topped with a timber castle, and formed the judicial and legislative centre for a large area of Buchan. A modern stone marker on a cairn states: 'Here the Moramers of Buchan held courts prior to 1214. On this site stood a motte and bailey castle, where the Norman Earls of Buchan 1214–1307 were installed in their titles and offices. From there they administered the province and dispensed justice, thus the site became known as Earl's Hill. It was from here that John Comyn, the last earl, gathered his followers to fight at the Battle of Barra in 1308.' Following defeat at Barra, Comyn and his forces were pursued by Edward Bruce, brother of King Robert the Bruce. Further lives were lost at Bruce Hill, Aikey Brae and Slains. The victorious Robert the Bruce took his revenge on the Comyn lands of Buchan, and it is said the area resembled a 'flaming torch' as a result. This event was known as the Harrying of Buchan, with Ellon 'reduced to a smouldering ruin, with its greatness and prosperity completely gone'. Phoenix-like the town rose again and strove towards social, economic and cultural development. Ellon suffered more at the hands of the so-called liberator than it ever did under the Comyns. In 1877 the North of Scotland Bank moved its premises from Old Bank House in the Square to Market Street.

Ythan Terrace. The Hon. William Gordon granted half-acre feus on the land by the Ythan, later to become Ythan Terrace, in the second decade of the nineteenth century. At the same time the area between here and what would become Station Road began to undergo expansion and development. Three blocks of three-storey buildings were put up on Ythan Terrace. The first one, just to the west of the Buchan Hotel, was built in 1815 and was made into flats in the 1920s. The second two blocks were finished in 1818. One was demolished after the First World War and the other went into commercial use. Rose Cottage was built on Ythan Terrace around 1818.

Pratt describes St Mary on the Rock as 'the architectural feature of Ellon', adding that it is 'a very handsome building in the Early English style, with a graceful little tower'. The church occupies a prominent spot on the south bank of the Ythan on the 'Craig' and was constructed in 1870 to designs by George Edmund Street, a noted Gothic architect, to replace a chapel built at Craighall in 1816 which had been deemed unsafe. By 26 June 1746 the backlash of Culloden was making life uncomfortable in Ellon, with the Episcopalian meeting house, which had been built near the parish church in 1713, burned down by government forces. Episcopalians, who were loyal Jacobite supporters, included members of Ellon's prominent families such as the Gordons of Ellon, the Turners of Turnerhall, and the Fullertons of Dudwick, and they were all under pressure because of their allegiances. The laird of Waterton, Thomas Forbes, was made to provide forage for the Duke of Cumberland's troops and laws were passed allowing the jailing of Episcopalian clergy, among them the noted poet-parson of Longside, the Revd John Skinner. Ellon folk sacrificed much in the rebellion. James Sutter (or Sutton), a local joiner, was an artilleryman and was captured and imprisoned at Carlisle, then Chester Castle, prior to being deported to the colonies. John Lowther of Ellon, and William Smith from Yonderton, Ellon, both served in the regiment of the Duke of Perth. John Lowther was captured and died in prison, but William Smith managed to escape. 46-year-old Alexander Wilkie, a labourer from Turnerhall, was captured and died at Tilbury Fort on the Thames estuary.

Like most towns in the country, Ellon was affected by the Disruption of 1843, the most notable schism in the history of the Church of Scotland. This involved many clergy and congregations breaking away from the Established Church to form the Free Church, in protest at the involvement of influential landowners in the appointment of ministers. In 1845 Ellon's Free Church congregation, comprising seven individuals, bought an old independent chapel, and this marked the beginnings of Ellon Free Church. The chapel was razed in 1856 and a church built in its place: its interior was renewed in 1896 at a cost of £600. Another breakaway group, the United Presbyterian Church (which originated from a Secession congregation formed in 1791), built a place of worship in 1894 on the north corner of Union Street at its junction with Station Road at a cost of £1,150 (the UP congregation had formerly worshipped in Ythan Terrace). In 1900 the United Presbyterian and Free Churches joined together to form the United Free Church, although the two congregations continued to worship separately before merging in 1905 as Ellon United Free Church, based in the Union Street building. The UF Church rejoined the Church of Scotland in 1929, at which point the church in Union Street became St Andrew's Church of Scotland (right), while the old parish church in the Square was called St Mary's Church of Scotland. In 1947 the two churches united to form a single Ellon Parish Church. St Andrews was sold in 1955 for £2,250 and became the County Cinema. It was later used as a furniture showroom but was subsequently demolished and houses built on the site. In September 1992 a Catholic church, Our Lady and St John the Baptist, was built in Union Street and dedicated by His Lordship Bishop Mario Conti.

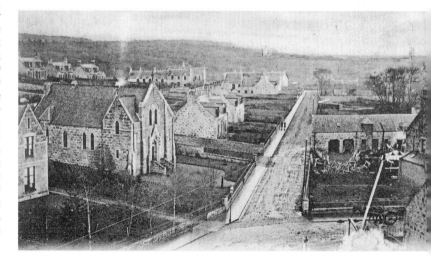

The congregation that was the forerunner of Ellon's United Presbyterian Church dated from 1791. It initially met at Auchmacoy, and in 1820 joined forces with another group of seceders, the Burgher New Lights, to become the Auchmacoy United Secession Church. They built a church in Ythan Terrace in 1827, and following the union of the Secession and Relief Churches in 1847 this became Ellon United Presbyterian Church. The congregation moved to a new church in Union Street in 1894, which became the United Free Church in 1900 after a further amalgamation. Subsequently the old church was used as a house ('Pluscarden') and furniture showroom. This picture shows the town's Established Church in Ythan Terrace.

In 1860 a railway bridge was built across the Ythan as part of the construction of the Formartine & Buchan Railway, but during completion of the masonry on the south side of the river soft clay below the foundations gave way and 'brought down the whole structure on a Sunday afternoon'. The opening of the railway on 18 July 1861 led to a major transformation of Ellon. It branched off the main Inverness to Aberdeen line at Dyce, running via Ellon to Fraserburgh, with branches from Maud Junction to Peterhead, Ellon to Cruden Bay and Boddam (1898), and Fraserburgh to St Combs. The line was laid about 1 km due west of Ellon, and had the effect of creating a new focus for development for the town. By 1895 the Station Hotel, a tannery, the hospital and two auction marts had sprung up along Station Road, underlining the commercial importance of this area, with attention shifting away from the Square for the first time. Prior to 1860 Auchterellon had been undeveloped apart from nurseries and crofts. Commodities transported by rail included cattle, draff from Speyside distilleries, coal, fertiliser, grain, potatoes, newspapers and mail. Trains of three or four coaches from Fraserburgh and Peterhead would join at Maud, while an additional few coaches from Boddam would be added at Ellon to make a decent-sized train to pull into Aberdeen Station. The stationmaster's house was built in 1865, and in 1919 was being occupied by John Ogston. By 1957 the building had become a signalman's house. The Buchan line was profitable up to the First World War, with limited alternatives for long journeys and military operations using it to freight coal to Peterhead for minesweepers and to service the Longside airship base. The Great North of Scotland Railway lost money on the Cruden Bay line, however, as it didn't prove to have the kudos of similar operations at Gleneagles and Turnberry run by other railways in conjunction with their hotels. At the height of the herring industry as many as nineteen fish specials a day might leave Fraserburgh for the south, and when the fleet sailed for Yarmouth and Lowestoft the female herring gutters followed in special trains from Fraserburgh and Peterhead. The motor bus, a major source of competition to the railway, made itself felt in Buchan from around 1923. Jimmy Sutherland of Peterhead charged 3s.6d. for a return fare from Peterhead to Aberdeen, substantially undercutting the railway which charged 10s. for the same trip.

The Second World War and the 1956 Suez crisis provided a temporary boost to Britain's railways, but Dr Beeching arrived on the scene in 1959 spelling the beginning of the end for many branch lines. Passenger services between Maud and Peterhead and Fraserburgh and St Combs came to a halt on 3 May 1965, although goods services to Peterhead continued until the Maud to Peterhead line closed completely on 7 September 1970. Passenger traffic to Fraserburgh ceased on 4 October 1965, but a daily goods train known as 'The Brocher' ran on the 47-mile track from Dyce Junction to Fraserburgh until 1979. The Brocher left from Craiginches goods yard, Aberdeen, picking up crew at Dyce signal box, after which the train had the line to itself. It carried parcels, fish and coal, making the 47-mile trip at a maximum speed of 45 mph. After Parkhill there was a 1 in 74 climb, while half a mile before Newmachar the line encountered a deep cutting at Hill of Strypes. This was susceptible to snow blockage, and a passenger train was stranded for twenty hours during blizzards in 1960. There was a 1 in 75 bank between Ellon and Arnage. In 1975–76 there was talk of relaying track to Inverugie to service oil and gas developments, but this came to nothing. The Buchan line's fate was sealed in 1979 when Grampian Regional Council's request for funding to support it was turned down, the costs being estimated at £100,000, with double that amount needed if the line was to accommodate heavier rolling stock such as fuel tankers. An enthusiasts' tour took place in April 1979, with stops at Ellon, Maud, Strichen and Fraserburgh, at which time Ellon's station buildings were in relatively good order. Having been closed, part of the Buchan line is now a walkway, with the bridges over Station Road and the New Deer road removed for safety.

Ellon's Station Hotel was built in 1891 with one wing constructed for – and kept for the exclusive use of – Sir James Gordon McDonald of Rhodesia when he was visiting the town. After his death his bedrooms were modified to become the hotel restaurant, while his public rooms downstairs became the lounge. An additional west wing was added in 1925. An 1895 advertisement for the Station Hotel read: 'Ellon, Aberdeenshire, The Station Hotel (in close proximity to Railway Station). Suites of Rooms for Private Families, and Families Boarded by the Week or Month. Tariff Moderate. Excellent Salmon and Trout Fishing on one of the best parts of the River Ythan at a Moderate Charge. Posting in all its Branches. Good Stabling Accommodation. Charles Lamont, Proprietor.'

The station buffet, marked 'Refreshments' here and simply called 'the Buffet', stood opposite Oliphant's signal box (named after a former signalman) about 100 yards from the Station Hotel. In an undated photograph it bears the sign 'Cassie, Station Buffet'. As its name suggests it was an eating establishment, but it was also used for dances and weddings. The Buffet was unlicensed, the drouthy having to adjourn to the Station Hotel, from where it was said that guests, generally men, had a habit of failing to return to the function in hand! As well as a dance hall and dining room, there was also a private room, kept for special occasions, for example for the use of the bride and groom at weddings. Staff apparently referred to this as the 'Spoonitarium'. Mart-day 'denner' (lunch) was on offer at the Buffet for farmers, the auctioneers apparently favouring Station Hotel fare. Bill Forbes was the last owner of the Buffet, and his widow Betty Forbes recalled that they served 'good plain, homely food – soup, stovies, and mince and tatties'. Mr and Mrs Forbes ran the Buffet together for 24 years prior to its sale. The premises were taken over by Fishing Hydraulics (Scotland) Ltd. in 1974, and the former Buffet building was used by them until 1985 when they built new premises on the site.

William Hardie & Sons were subcontracted by the council to build and repair roads before these activities became the direct responsibility of a council department. The firm's vehicles could also be seen at Regent Quay, Aberdeen, transporting coal brought in by boat. As the name suggests, steam wagons such as this one did not have an internal combustion engine, instead using high-pressure steam for propulsion. They were economical and had a long lifespan, and at least one was brought back into use at Aberdeen Harbour during the 1957 Suez fuel crisis. In addition to their transport and contracting business, the Hardie family farmed at Denebank.

Station Road. The first signs of Ellon's expansion to the west came in the second decade of the nineteenth century when William Gordon of Ellon Castle granted half-acre feus from Ythan Terrace to Langley Road (later to become Station Road). Broomhead on Station Road was built around this time. The arrival of the railway in 1861 opened up the area around the station as a commercial centre, shifting attention from the Square. Well-to-do Aberdonians subsequently built handsome villas along Station Road, which linked the Square with the station, using these as summer residences. Many are built in a style typical of the period in the north-east, featuring much more elaborate stonework than found on earlier dwellings.

Station Road. Between 1845 and 1847 Longley Cottage was built on the south side of Station Road as a home for James Black, factor to the Ellon Estate, and was subsequently used by his successor, Thomas F. Jamieson. From the 1900s to the late 1940s development continued to be focused to the north and west of the centre of Ellon. This meant that the Square became isolated on the periphery of the town, rather than occupying its centre as had been the original intention.

Station Road was previously called Langley or Longley Road. Thomas Mann's shop included a millinery department, and hats were clearly the order of the day for ladies going about their business in Ellon.

Victoria Hall was built in 1901 and stands on the south side of Station Road. The feu which it occupies formed part of the old public park. Architecturally, the hall is said to be an example of the late perpendicular or Tudor Gothic style. It is made of pink granite and was built to accommodate 800 people, also housing a public library at one time in one of several ground floor rooms, an initiative of the Ellon Mutual Improvement Association.

The education committee of Aberdeen County Council took over running of the library within the Victoria Hall and its 2,000 volumes in 1939. Today the library is sited in Station Road in a purpose-built facility, having previously occupied temporary accommodation.

The Square seen on 22 June 1911, the coronation day of George V and Queen Mary. To celebrate the occasion a parade met in the Square before processing along Station Road, and included a pony with a monkey on its back. The suitably attired monkey had been imported from South America by the son of a local horse dealer, Francis Catto of Knockothie. Butcher George Ruxton, dressed as John Bull, led the parade. Horse-drawn lorries represented the town's different trades. Carts were freshly painted and decorated with bunting, and horses were turned out in their finery, including home-made crepe paper roses. Butchers Charles Kidd, William Wood, George Ruxton and William Reid were represented, as well as local tailors, and there were also carts belonging to Chrystall's, normally used for coal and feedstuff deliveries. Young men in hunting attire, hunting horns at the ready, were in attendance, while others joined in with bikes. Meanwhile pupils of Ellon Higher Grade School, each with a white enamel mug on a string around their neck, lined up to await the whistle that would allow them to begin their ordered march to watch the historic event. A picnic was organised in a field in Station Road with races for both children and single and married ladies. The latter weren't well-attired for the event, wearing starched white blouses, straight ankle-length boots, skirts with cinched-in waists and giant hats.

McDonald Park lies to the north of Ellon town centre and covers 67 acres, 28 of which are taken up by woodland, with the remainder comprising McDonald Park golf course. Former Ellon Academy pupils will remember the park well as its paths were used as a cross-country course and distance running was an enforced aspect of physical education. The park was gifted to the town by Sir James Gordon McDonald, KCB, OBE, 1867–1943. He was a pupil at the local school, then attended Gordon's College, Aberdeen, before enjoying a distinguished career in South Africa. In 1919 he purchased land which had originally formed part of Ellon Castle's estate and used this to lay out a golf course and plant woodland. Having built a retirement home for his parents on part of it, Sir James then laid out the park. He engaged the services of Stewart Burns, golf professional at Cruden Bay, to design the 9-hole golf course, and the opening ceremony took place on 1 June 1927. Just over a year later, Sir James gifted the park and golf course to the council to hold in trust for the people of Ellon. The feu-superiority rights were transferred to Dr Barnardo's Homes for Children, but purchased by Gordon District Council in 1990. After his retirement Sir James Gordon divided his time between Ellon and Rhodesia, living at the Station Hotel while in Ellon. During the Second World War he joined the Home Guard and served as an intelligence officer, despite then being in his seventies. He lost his life when the vessel he was sailing to South Africa on in 1942, SS *Ceramic*, was torpedoed by a German submarine.

Ellon Bowling Club is located in Union Street. Proposals for a bowling green and associated club were put forward at a public meeting at the Lower Victoria Hall on 17 October 1906. A committee was duly formed and set about fund-raising through events such as bazaars, going on to obtain a site, source turf and build a pavilion. The green was opened on Wednesday 4 June 1914 by Mr Gordon of Ellon, and the club's first president was Andrew Cairns of Esslemont. The Ellon club joined the Aberdeen & District Bowling Association in 1920, becoming part of the new Buchan Bowling Association in 1921. The first jack of the season was traditionally bowled by the wife of the president, but initially ladies were not able to play bowls, instead being restricted to preparing teas with home bakes as required. However, a ladies section opened in 1961. In the early 1970s there was talk of moving the green to make way for the Ellon Academy extension, but an alternative site in the castle grounds was chosen for this instead. Since its opening the pavilion has undergone a variety of improvements, and the green is now floodlit to extend the outdoor playing season. In 2003 the club had 54 female members, 90 men and four juniors.

From 1560, under the influence of John Knox, education became the responsibility of the church, and as in many other parishes Ellon's schoolmasters are listed in the church records. In 1620 the town's school was described as a 'grammer and musik scuill'. The fees were 13s.4d. Scots per quarter for reading and writing, with music costing an extra 20s. per quarter. The schoolmaster's salary, meanwhile, was a promised five bolls of meal and 6s.8d. in cash. The 'Stone House' was built in 1543 by Gilbert Annand of Auchterellon on the banks of the Ythan, off the Square, and became the school and school-house in 1651, serving as such for 225 years, during which time many modifications were made. It was subsequently converted to a dwelling house. In the nineteenth century the schoolmaster was Dr John Davidson, a noted scholar who became the first actuary of Ellon Savings Bank. After 1843, a Free Church school became part of the school, while a Sessional school was also in existence. Local school boards were introduced in 1872, after which the new premises seen here were constructed on Bridge Street, at which point all three original schools closed. Ellon Public School (later Ellon Academy) opened on 22

May 1876 and comprised six classrooms, three for boys and three for girls. Boys' and girls' education seems to have been organised entirely separately, with records only being kept for the boys (education of girls, one presumes, being considered less important). An entry from the log dated 19 October 1877 indicates the importance of farming to the area at the time: 'The harvest is not finished and the numbers are still small'. Educational standards were monitored by school inspectors, and on 13 August 1880 it was recorded: 'The papers given in by the scholars in English Literature show that scarcely anything beyond the mere repetition of the lines has been successfully attempted'. Five years later, on 14 August 1885, it was noted that 'The school is conducted with fidelity and vigour. The infants have made satisfactory progress in the elements of Reading, Writing and Number. The infant classroom provides floor space for 36. The average attendance in this room during the past quarter has been 73.' From 1885 boys and girls were taught together, a new headmaster having been appointed. That year the school roll was 372 and the building still comprised six classrooms. In 1899 there were 487 pupils, and by then a new higher grade department had been added without any expansion of the accommodation. A further two classrooms were subsequently built, and an additional storey was added between 1909 and 1911. Further building work took place in the late 1930s when the headmaster's house was demolished and seven large classrooms and a gymnasium were added. Following the Second World War, new classrooms were constructed at the back of the building, with the secondary department warranting the appointment of principal teachers for English, maths, science and other subjects. The school coat of arms was granted in 1951 by the Lord Lyon, King of Arms. Its motto, *Famam Extendite Factis*, means 'Extend your Reputation by Deeds'. The final set of extensions to this building dated from between 1963 and 1966, when the facade was altered with the removal of the bell tower. In the late 1970s an additional school building and adjoining community centre, including a swimming pool, was built in the grounds of Ellon Castle, creating 'old' and 'new' academy buildings with pupils crossing Bridge Street between classes. Discussions are currently ongoing about future provision to accommodate all pupils on one site, and how to meet the educational needs of a town whose population continues to expand, along with that of its hinterland. Separate primary schools now exist to serve the Auchterellon and Meiklemill areas.

An 1867 medical officer's report recorded that of 'the great numbers of accidents, fever and diphtheria [cases] sent to Aberdeen Infirmary, that very few have recovered is attributed to the great distance they have to be removed'. Local medical facilities were seen as the means by which to tackle illnesses such as cholera, typhoid, scarlet fever, diphtheria and smallpox, and in 1888 the Gordon Hospital for Infectious Diseases was built by the parochial board at a cost of *c.*£800 in what then became Hospital Road. The hospital had seven beds and was run by Mr and Mrs Cumming, the latter serving as the matron, while her husband was a labourer. Their remuneration was a rent-free, furnished house 'with fire, light and soap'. Mrs Cumming also received one shilling a day 'when there [were] patients'. Twelve years on, the hospital had been extended to accommodate 39 patients and the following year a cab was converted to serve as an ambulance wagon. Hospital provision was free for patients with infectious diseases, although it was noted by the district committee clerk that 'still some patients have a great dread of it'. The hospital was later extended again, introducing maternity facilities in 1939. Despite much support for maintaining a local maternity unit – including a 2,000-strong petition and a plea from the ladies of Cairnnorrie Women's Rural Institute – the hospital closed in 1965.

Some of the houses in Ellon's Foresters Terrace were owned by Auchmacoy Estate, but the terrace is thought to have been built by the Ancient Order of Foresters, a friendly society. The Johnston family lived at No. 3 Foresters Terrace until 1979, having moved there from a cottar house at Mains of Auchterellon prior to the Second World War. Members of the family were employed at the Station Buffet, the local florists and by the council. The house comprised two bedrooms, a toilet, and a kitchen-come-living room, all located off a long lobby. There were fireplaces in the living room and bedrooms. Alexander's the bakers was nearby, and the children made a slide on the brae in icy weather. Behind the terrace was a plant nursery and florists, with gardens and wash-houses to the front. Nearby there was a slaughterhouse, owned by Reid the butcher, the livestock pens for which can be seen in the foreground. Stringent legislation has now forced the closure of small local slaughterhouses throughout Buchan, and Mr Reid has since built a house on the site.

Auchtercrag, which stands on Gareta Hill set back from Commercial Road, was built in 1894 for William Smith, owner of the boot factory with the high chimney seen to the right. William Smith came from Newmachar and had previously owned another factory in Ellon, occupying the site of the *Ellon Times* office on Bridge Street and extending to where Salvo's now stands in Market Street. Both the factory and Auchtercrag were sold not long after 1894, with a John Milne buying the house. The McLaren brothers took over the boot factory in 1904, employing twenty people producing heavy farm boots under the brand 'The Clan'. A lighter boot was also made for Kingseat and Cornhill Hospitals. Machinery at the factory was steam-driven and electricity was generated using a coal-fired boiler and steam engine. The start of the working day was marked by a hooter sounding at 7.45 a.m., and this was also to be heard at lunchtime and the end of the working day. Clan boots were made of heavy-duty waterproof leather with iron heels, toe plates and tackets on the soles to make them hard-wearing. They were marketed to shops in the Gordon district, Deeside, Alford, Laurencekirk and Fife, but unfortunately the Wellington boot was to trample on the McLaren brothers' business prospects and the factory had to cut back. After changing hands several times, Auchtercrag was bought by Gordon District Council in 1987, by which time it had not been occupied for some time and required some attention. It has since been restored and many original features have been incorporated into the Auchtercrag Mansion development which comprises seven flats. A residential home for the elderly now occupies the site of the boot factory.

The Chestnuts, Ellon.

Sir James Reid was Queen Victoria's physician and lived in the Chestnuts, Ellon. His son, Sir Edward Reid, bought Ellon Castle in 1929. Sir James was also doctor to Edward VII and George V and it is said that Queen Victoria appreciated his prescription of kale as a laxative. In the second half of 1914, Sir James was called to Scapa Flow where Prince Albert (later King George VI) was serving with the grand fleet. He was taken to Aberdeen for surgery, and during his recovery visited the Chestnuts on several occasions. The house sits in a prominent position on Bridge Street where it crosses Station Road.

The chief estate within the parish of Logie Buchan is Auchmacoy, situated on the north side of the Ythan. The mansion seen here was built *c*.1835 by James Buchan of Auchmacoy (d.1874). The Buchans are descendants of the noted Comyn family, who ruled the district prior to the reign of Robert the Bruce, and Auchmacoy estate has been in their hands for some considerable time. It is recorded in at least one source that the Comyn who owned Auchmacoy stayed faithful to Bruce and the political aim of Scottish independence, and was consequently given leave to keep the lands on the understanding that he changed his name. He did this, taking on the name of the district he lived in, Buchan. The family's ownership of the lands was confirmed in 1503 by James IV, who granted a new charter to Andrew Buchan of Auchmacoy. Major-General Thomas Buchan was a prominent member of the family who gave distinguished service with Charles II and James VII. At one time there were two chapels on the Auchmacoy Estate: 'at the Dovecot of Auchmacoy, and at the Old Yard of Auchmacoy, both for the use of the Buchans of Auchmacoy. . . . At Denhead of Auchmacoy there is a fine Mission Hall, erected in memory of the late Mrs Buchan' (*The Vale of Ythan*). Pratt describes Auchmacoy as follows: 'The house, admirably situated, is built in the Elizabethan style, and forms a striking object in the landscape. The ground to the westward slopes gently to the margin of a little stream, and forms a beautiful lawn, embellished with clumps of trees and shrubs; and to the north rises to a gentle eminence, thickly clothed with woods. On the south and east, the house overlooks a steep glen, tastefully laid out and cut into walks. Beyond this is seen the noble sweep of the basin formed by the Ythan, with the sea in the distance. A finer situation can hardly be imagined.'

Esselmont Estate lies about two miles west of Ellon. Originally held by the Celtic Moramers of Buchan, it then passed to the Comyns, Norman Earls of Buchan, and was linked with Arnage, another local estate, until 1516. From 1381 Esselmont was owned by the Cheyne family, who also held Arnage and Straloch. The 10th Cheyne laird died in 1631 and Esslemont then passed to the Forbes and Hay families. There were 203 tenants and sub-tenants on the Esslemont lands in 1696, and seven servants were employed at the Castle of Esslemont (the ruins of which stand by the B9004 near Mains of Esslemont). In 1706 the Barony of Esslemont was purchased by Bailie James Gordon of Ellon Castle. Robert Gordon of Hallhead bought it in 1728, and the granite mansion house seen here dates from 1868. In 1958 Esslemont was recorded as belonging to Captain Robert Wolridge Gordon, 21st Laird of Hallhead and 10th of Esslemont, and it remains in Gordon hands today under the stewardship of Charles Gordon.

Turner Hall is named in fulfilment of the wish, detailed in his will, of John Turner of Birse, merchant in Danzig, to immortalise his name. He additionally made bequests for educational and charitable purposes, one of which benefited Marischal College. John Turner's executors purchased the Barony of Rosehill, formerly Hilltown, and in 1694 the lands of Tipperty, all of which were subsequently combined as the Barony of Turnerhall. In 1861 the sixth laird constructed what was said to be 'a striking if not very attractive house of two storeys with gabled wings, deep eaves, round-headed double and tripartite windows and a four storey square entrance-tower, off centre and slightly institutionalised'. This was demolished in 1933, although its walled gardens and kennels survived. Of note is the windmill, sited at Hilton of Turnerhall, thought to date from either 1787 or 1825. The sails of the mill were said to have blown off on 28 December 1879 in the same storm that had such a devastating effect on the Tay Bridge. Following this, the windmill was capped and a three-horse gin was installed in front of the tower to power the adjacent threshing barn. Subsequent progress was represented by a stationary engine in the base of the tower. This was later the source of a fire that consumed the original timber-work and fittings of the windmill.

39

This picture shows stooks of sheaves in a park outside Ellon. Originally the harvest was cut by scythe and the sheaves had to be made by hand, using lengths of straw to form a band to hold them together. In Buchan oats (known locally as corn) once formed the main crop. Before the introduction of combine harvesters, a degree of automation was introduced in the form of binders, which gathered the crop into sheaves but left the grain attached to the straw. The sheaves were then arranged in stooks (stacks), allowing the harvest to dry off until it could be gathered in. Stooks were made to point north to south, rather than east/west, to protect them from the weather, and farmers would use a landmark to align them. The harvest was taken in using horse-drawn carts (tractors in later years), and the sheaves were then built up into a ruck at the steading. Harvest was both a time of anxiety as to whether the weather would be kind, and a period of back-breaking toil.

Ulaw is a farm in Ellon Parish. Here two cattle, Charlie and Jock, are yoked to the plough, rather than the more usual pair of Clydesdales. It was also known for a cow to be yoked alongside a horse. In the background are two rucks, which were built from sheaves of oats taken in from the fields after harvest. This was the means of storing the harvest and good ruck-building was imperative to keep the straw and grain safe for later use. Folk building the rucks would have the sheaves forked to them from workers below. It was then their job to place and pack them properly. The ruck was fastened down with a natural binding material, often made of rushes, which had been twined together into a sort of rope using thraw heuks, also used for making rope. The twine would be rolled into a ball, called a cloo, and thrown up to the workers on top of the ruck to undertake the fastening down. The ruck had to stay fast until threshing time, when a steam-powered threshing mill would visit and the grain and straw was separated and used for human and animal food and animal bedding. The chaff was also separated and used to stuff mattresses, making a chaff or 'calf' bed. The visit of the threshing mill (thrashin' mull) was also a time of great neighbourly co-operation. Womenfolk helped with the manual labour, but also had the challenge of providing a 'stem mull denner' for a large and hungry workforce.

The farm of New Craig lies in the Parish of Udny and is one of three farms to be found on rising ground called the Craig. New Craig sits on the south side. Its neighbour Old Craig was said to have once had 8,800 yards of dry stane dyke. Each yard of dyke would generally have contained two or three cart-loads of stone weighing a ton or more, adding up to as much as 26,000 tons of stone in total. This would have represented a huge number of man-hours for both stone-gathering and dyke-building.

Auchterellon Mains, or Mains of Auchterellon, formed part of the Auchterellon Estate. It comprised 407 acres and Thomas Moreis was listed as being the tenant from 1590 to 1606, at which period there was a 'glasin-wright' (glazier) at Auchterellon. Living at the manor house in 1696 was Laird Robert Udny, his wife Elizabeth Fullerton, and their three daughters and two sons. There were also eight servants, while Janet Hutchone is mentioned as occupying the tavern. This was situated on the west side of the New Deer road, opposite the Hornhillock to Broomfield road. When the last tavern-keeper, Sophia Burnett, died in the 1880s the building was made into a double cottar house for Mains of Auchterellon. Horse-power was of course paramount on Buchan farms until the advent of tractors, and the ploughman had considerable status in the community. There was great competition on and between farms as to who could plough the best and straightest furrows, with ploughing matches remaining part of the farming calendar to this day. The ploughman also had to be a skilled horseman and there was a tradition of a secret horseman's society. When deemed by experienced horsemen to be of sufficient maturity, a young man on a farm would be initiated into the society via a Masonic type ritual, sometimes receiving a single horse hair on his pillow on his eighteenth birthday as a bidding to attend the ritual. It was said that he got 'the horseman's grippin word'. The young man had to bring bread and whisky to the ceremony, and if he kept his nerve and was admitted successfully the secrets of the horseman were shared with him, under strict oath. He was then allowed to take a pair of horse, graduating from 'the orra beast' (a single horse used by the 'orra loon' to do odd jobs around the farm), and the farmer was expected to pay him a full horseman's wage (*The Horseman's Word*).

Backhill, Knockhall, lies towards Newburgh within that parish. This picture shows a typical scene on a north-east farm during the early twentieth century, with a pair of Clydesdale horses being used to till the soil. The horses' coats seem to gleam, and certainly their health and welfare would have been of paramount importance to the prosperity of the farm. Work on a Buchan farm was hard, with the horses being fed and cared for before the men had their breakfast, probably of brose. 'Denner' time was 12 o'clock on the dot, and allowed sufficient time for the horses to rest. At the end of the day the horses would again be fed before the men went in for their supper. On farms where several men were employed there was a hierarchy, the first horseman getting access to the water trough with his pair before the others. It was also important for a fee'd man to be employed by a farmer who had able horses. The disappointment of a poor choice is recorded in this Buchan bothy ballad:

The Barnyards o' Delgaty

He promised me the ae best pair,
I ever set my e'en upon;
Fin I gaed hame ti the Barnyards,
There wis naething there bit skin an
    bone.

The aul balck horse sat on his
    rump,
The aul fite meer lay on her wime,
An' a' that I could hup an cry,
They widna rise at yokin' time.

It was noted by a horse dealer from the south that in Buchan the traditional diet was porridge, oatcakes and brose, all made from oats. On his return home he said 'They feed the men in Buchan the same as we feed our horses'. A gem of a rhyme attributed to north-east people is: 'A farting man's the man to hire, A farting horse will never tire' (*The Latter Day Horse Dealers*).

While donkeys may have been used to pull carts or as a means of transport, this practice was much less common than it was in Ireland, and they didn't play a large part in Buchan farming. Instead donkeys were sometimes kept as pets, or used to help develop a youngster's equine knowledge and experience. This photograph was taken by William Hutcheon of Tipperty near Ellon suggesting a local connection.

This view of Ellon from the south shows part of the town's rural hinterland. According to sixteenth, seventeenth and eighteenth century records, Ellon folk endured centuries of civil troubles and social unrest, coupled with less than satisfactory cattle-rearing and agricultural systems. Famine was a constant threat, with a stubborn reluctance to relinquish old-fashioned farming techniques such as infield and outfield cropping. Particularly hard times were recorded in 1578 and 1614, with a 'continewance of ye evill wedder in ye harvest tyme' during the latter year. Conditions were wet and stormy in 1621 with 'ye wattirs and burns gryt', and there were floods and heavy snowfalls in 1624. From 1687 to 1700 'dire famine stalked the land'. Crops failed in 1739 and 1740, while in 1741 the 'clamant circumstances of the country' are noted, events which prompted the Provost of Aberdeen to write to the Presbytery of Ellon 'desiring a fifth part of what meal the several members can spare after serving their own families for behoof of the town of Aberdeen'. 1742, by contrast, saw a plentiful harvest. The years 1782–3 were said to be the worst in Ellon's history, with people and livestock dying in their hundreds. Godsman describes this period as 'the culmination of the stubborn opposition of the tenant farmer to change'. Many farmers, farm-workers and even lairds left the area, moving further afield within Scotland or emigrating to seek fresh opportunities. During 1782, 'the snowy hairst', Ellon kirk session provided food for 110 householders in dire straits. By 1792 there were only 190 people living in Ellon with a total population of 1,830 within the parish boundaries. Following this period there was eventually a gradual adoption of better farming methods, with livestock genetics improved by beasts from further afield and new crops and improved seeds introduced.

The figure in the boat was the well-known local character, 'Boatie Tam' Pirie, who lived at Boat of Fechil, Ellon, and died in 1992 aged 81. With few bridges in Scotland before the eighteenth century, ferries were common, and Boat of Logie, Boat of Fechil and Boat of Ardlethen were all ferry crossing points on the Ythan. Boatie Tam was Ellon's last ferryman, and almost up to the time of his death he crossed the Ythan in the same fashion as his mother and grandfather had done before him. He resisted 'newfangled' inventions such as electricity and hot running water, saying 'I dinna really want it'. It was only in his latter years that he accepted having water piped into his cottage. Tam spent his latter days at Ythanvale nursing home, where he confessed he enjoyed the luxury. His cottage has now been restored and upgraded as a weekend family retreat. Tam's grandfather worked the ferry at Logie, while his mother, Boatie Mary, oared a coble at Fechil where she lived by the Ythan. She was said to have had 'an enquiring mind and carrying voice'. She also tended the croft and reared a family. The ferry fare was a penny, but the postman, packman, minister and laird were all carried at no charge. Cottar-folk often paid in kind with a jar of jam or a rabbit for the pot. Boatie Tam took over the oars from his mother, and his death marked the end of an era. When the need for ferrymen ceased, Tam was employed by the LNER and later British Rail. He recalled a fierce Buchan winter in 1942 when the Ythan froze over and trains were trapped in blizzards.

The Ythan bisects the Parish of Ellon and is fed by a network of tributaries: the Ebrie from the Hill of·Corsegight in New Deer; the Bronie Burn, Hill of Blair; and the Yowlie, Modley and Auchmacoy Burns. Peat mosses were once a feature of the parish, but have been drained and are now cultivated. These included Moss of Ellon, Moss Neuk and Moss Side. The famed Jamie Fleeman, servant of the Laird of Udny and termed the Laird o' Udny's feel (fool) and something of a character, was a frequent visitor to Ellon. It is said that he once watched a gentleman he disliked sizing up the ford between Fechil and Waterton, and was then asked by him where was best to cross. When the horse and gentleman found themselves out of their depth Fleeman was accused of putting them in danger. His response was 'Gosh be here! I've seen the geese and dyeuks hunners of times crossin' there, an I'm sure your horse has langer legs than the dyeukes or the geese either!'

Even in the fifteenth century the village of Newburgh was a busy port, handling mainly wool and timber. It levied lower charges than Aberdeen, with the result that in 1573 Aberdeen Town Council took action and confiscated the village's sails, thus immobilising Newburgh's shipping fleet. The village was well positioned to trade in lime and other fertilisers which were imported into the surrounding farming area, and also to ship out locally produced grain. However, the Ythan's mouth and the sharp bends of the estuarine channel made the passage of vessels of any size tricky. In 1844 a wooden jetty was built by the Aberdeen Lime Company at Inches – prior to that loading and unloading had to be done at low water. Gibb reported in 1819 that 'those who have to bring grain from a distance or carry away lime, coal etc., being little accustomed to calculate tides, frequently come at inopportune times and there wait with little detention and have their horses much injured by being obliged to keep them standing in water whilst the carts are loaded and unloaded on to the vessels.' The 300-foot pier allowed freight to be transferred relatively efficiently to and from ships, lighters and small barges. In 1845 George Cruden noted that 'lighters, carrying from six to twelve tons now ply up and down with the tide, aided when the wind is favourable, by a sail, and always by a set (or pole) twenty feet long, in the handle of the lightermen. Eight or nine of these, belonging to the shipowners of Newburgh, are employed in carrying lime, coals and bones to different landing places on the banks of the river, the highest of which is about four miles from its mouth.' Prior to the end of the nineteenth century, barges were towed upstream from Newburgh quay to the Meadows at Ellon by the paddle tug *Despatch*. Such a paddle tug is pictured here, with barges behind. By 1890 much of the river trade was centred on Mitchell & Rae's milling works at Newburgh quay and the jetty of the Aberdeen Lime Company. Even a small paddle tug, requiring just over a metre of water, would have been obliged to sail upstream to Ellon on an incoming tide, and there are frequent records of the *Despatch* being grounded.